Medical Qi Gong after Prof. Wu Zhong Hu

Exercises to maintain and improve the Health

Editor, co-author and photos:
Alternative practitioner
Hartmut von Czapski, Xanten

Medical
Qi Gong
after Prof. Wu Zhong Hu

Imprint
Bibliographic information from the German National Library:
The German National Library lists this publication in the
German National Bibliography; detailed bibliographical data
can be found on the Internet at http://dnb.dnb.de.
© 2019 Hartmut von Czapski
Production and publishing: BoD - Books on Demand,
Norderstedt
ISBN: 9783751904575

Content

Prof. Wu, Zhong Hu

He was:

Director of the Qigong Research Committee Shanghai
Director of the prevention and treatment department for tumor diseases (especially pancreas and liver tumors) of the Qigong Research Department in Shanghai
Director of the Shanghai Research Center for Rehabilitation Medicine
Qi Gong doctor of China's Scientific and Technological Association
Adviser and lecturer to the Qigong and Ciaoly Committee
Specially tested Qigong Master Shanghai No. 9029
Creator of the 8 Qigong exercises for self-regulation

What is Qi Gong? An introduction

Qi Gong is a peculiarity of Chinese culture. In Qing Hai, Datong a clay jug with colorful representations of dancers was found. The archaeologists found that these come from the Majia-yao culture. That was 5000 years ago. The experts believe that this is the origin of Qi Gong. It comes from the people. Workers who struggled with diseases for life invented methods and exercises for self-healing of body and soul. In the beginning, the different positions were probably based on an imitation of animal movements. If these assumptions are correct, the origin can be dated back even further.

Although there are different forms of Qi Gong today, e.g. Play- Qigong, Wu Shu, hard and light Qigong, it is clear that the origin is in therapeutic Qigong. Over the years, the Qi Gong has changed and it continues to change and improve. Qi Gong is a very subtle treatment. In the past there was not our scientific knowledge, but different religions.

The faithful of these religions also practiced various Qigong methods.
Med. Qi Gong founded the Chinese medical theory. Qi Gong is a phenomenon so far, but it is also a branch of science. A physical science of self-inquiry. Several critical researches show that Qi Gong has great potential for maintaining health. Many Qigong phenomena have not yet been scientifically explained, but that doesn't mean,that these phenomena don't exist. One can only say that there remains an unsolved remnant.

There are certainly successes through Qi Gong, but one should not exaggerate them. Nor can you say that you can treat all (100) diseases with it. Different Qigong exercises are intended for different illnesses and nevertheless it is often advisable to seek additional help from a doctor or naturopath.

The med. Qi Gong is good for strengthening the body, treating diseases, maintaining health and prolonging life. It strengthens the constitution.

History of the med. Qi Gong
It is said that during the Tang-Yao period, 4000 years ago, there was a flood disaster in central China. The ruler Da Ju fought the water. The people who worked a lot in the damp and wet got stiff muscles and joints. Some people made hand and foot movements to relax the muscles, strengthen the bones, and stimulate blood circulation.

This drove away the moisture and cold and the pain subsided. This is called the original method Dao Yin of med. Qi Gong. The earliest and most complete description of breathing exercises can be found in the period of the Warring States (475-221 BC). The "Qi River Jade Inscription" consists of 54 words and is engraved on a twelve-sided jade cylinder.

In the classic of the yellow emperor "Nei Jing" from the time of the fighting empires, it is written: "Serene and desireless (to be), real energy in the river, keep the mind inside, then no illness comes. With breathing Qi (to absorb), focus on yourself, hold your mind, relax all muscles. " These two sentences clarify the content of the old Qi Gong .

So far there are over 10,000 different Qigong methods.
There are research institutes in several large Chinese cities such as Beijing and Shanghai to use modern technology to investigate the mechanism of action of Qi Gong.

The Shanghai Hypertension Research Institute published works with reports on changes that Qi Gong causes in the EKG and EEG in 1978. Work has also been published on how our sympathetic nervous system, which is overactive due to constant stress, achieves relaxation by predominating the parasympathetic nervous system through Qi Gong.

There are also tumor follow-up groups in the research institute as well as research on the stimulating effects of Qi Gong on the immune system.
There are 2 Qi Gong institutes in Beijing and Shanghai and there is a Qi Gong association in each city. Some T.C.M. (Traditional Chinese Medicine) Universities have a Qi Gong faculty. Qi Gong spreads from China all over the world.

Teachers give guest lectures abroad and exchange experiences. This situation is a good sign.

Definition of the term Qi Gong

The two words Qi Gong are rarely found in old books on medicine or sports. The content of Qi Gong is known in popular, religious medicine and martial arts. There were different forms with different goals, e.g. B. to protect public health, to make immortality pills to achieve deep meditation, as part of Kung Fu and Dao Yin (guiding Qi with movement).

In general, you can say that Qi Gong is a method of training your mind and body independently. The methods and theories have been developed over many generations by the ancestors in order to protect themselves from diseases and to prolong life.

As a med. Qi Gong is considered the triple regulating method at the Shanghai Qigong Institute.
The mind (heart), body and breathing regulation to train body and mind (heart) yourself.
Exercise can strengthen the body's defenses and improve self-regulation.

A peculiarity of Qi Gong as a practice method is that you have to enter an inner practice state. Posture and movements and breathing work together, mind and body are relaxed or tense, thoughts are concentrated and used. All this strengthens and regulates every organ function and stimulates the body's energy potential. The effect is keeping the body healthy, preventing illness and a long life.

<u>What is Qi?</u>
It is a substance that you normally cannot see and grope, but can feel. Our ancient philosophers thought that qi was a substance that originated in the Big Bang.
According to our Chinese Medicin Qi is perceived as a continuously moving and active substance, the basic substance from which the body arises. Qi maintains human life functions. Qi in Qi Gong is defined as an "essence" substance in the body with a certain energy. Qi can be formed, developed, transformed and moved in the body. In my decades of experience, Qi is an energy that can be controlled by the will, but it is also a carrier field with different information. With Qi Gong at a high level you can see the shape and color of Qi. There is Qi with different properties around every substance.

<u>What to consider when practicing</u>
Qigong exercises come in several levels, from low to high levels. The requirements for the regulation of body, breath, and mind are not the same. At different levels there are different important points.
In the initial stage, it is posture regulation.
In the second stage it is breath regulation.
In the third stage it is mind regulation.
In the intermediate level, body and breath regulation are equally important, mental regulation less so.

In the upper level, mind regulation is most important. Breath regulation is the second most important, body regulation is the least important or is no longer needed. The correct application of the triple regulation influences the success of the exercise.

The triple regulation
a) posture; correct wrong posture. Cooperation of relaxation and tension, the right balance between tense and loose muscles (loose should dominate);
b) Cooperation between posture and breathing regulation. Fine, deep, slow, long, calm, regular abdominal breathing should be achieved;
c) "Heart regulation". Guidance and unification.

Eliminate all distracting thoughts. One thought instead of 1000 thoughts. Inside look (Nei She). Meditation. Concentration inwards, at a certain point. A calm and relaxed psyche.
Concentrate on yourself. Not through external forces, but through independent practice, regulating and changing the body and the Qi flow with the aim of strengthening the body and protecting against diseases.

According to traditional Chinese medicine, body and psyche belong together and form a whole. In this way, the seven emotions (annoy, anger, fear, sadness, frustration, worry and excessive joyful excitement) are assigned to certain meridians and can cause a disturbance in the meridian and vice versa a disturbance in the meridian can affect the emotions.
Mind and body are one. When practicing qigong, you train both together.

In this book, exercises are listed that have excellent effects on the following symptoms, among others: for high and low blood pressure, stomach and intestinal complaints, indigestion, lung problems, insomnia, lack of concentration, cervical spine syndrome, back pain and excessive stress.

With regular and persistent practice of Qi Gong, practitioners can improve their health and find inner peace and relaxation.
Since the exercises can be carried out with different levels of effort, they are also suitable for weakened and older people.

1)Exercise with the palms of your hands to build up an energy field

- Relax standing or sit down, breathe naturally, keep your palms 10 cm apart, stay there for a moment

- Remove palms very slowly from each other up to 60 cm away(beginn with 30 cm), inhaling while doing so

- Slowly bring the palms together again (without touching), exhale as you do so

- Focus on the palms, feeling what you feel between the palms (e.g. magnetism, warmth, tingling, etc.)

- Bend your upper body back slightly as you inhale and bend forward as you exhale.

- Put your hands on unhealthy areas on your body or just on your breast and under your belly with a thin distance. Feel the energy of your hands.

Explanation of the exercise: According to traditional Chinese medicine, energy channels (called meridians) run from the fingers to the internal organs. As soon as you feel tingling, warmth, etc. in your hands, you will:

a) the circulation of blood and energy is also stimulated in the internal organs, blockages can be released;
b) an energy field built up in the hands;
c) the body's energy potential is raised and strengthened.
49 times

1   Energiefeld aufbauen   2

3

2) Harmonize the kidney and heart meridians

The palms of your hands point to the back of your feet, hands and arms move slowly up and down, breathing naturally.
When inhaling, the upper body moves slightly backwards, the hands are slowly moved upwards.

When exhaling, the upper body moves forward slightly, the hands are slowly moved downwards. Focus on the palms of the hands during the exercise.

Explanation of the exercise; When the hands are lifted up, yin energy (cooling energy) is drawn up, when moving down pathogenic, used energy is conducted down through the soles of the feet into the ground.
This exercise harmonizes the cardiac and renal meridian (stage fright, cardiac arrhythmia, insomnia, inner restlessness).
It strengthens the energy circulation, calms down by releasing tension downwards.

- 49 times -

1   Herz-Nieren-Übung

2

3

3) Standing exercise to absorb energy

Relax your upper body, breathe naturally, relax, don't think about anything. Bend your knees, feet parallel and shoulder-width apart.
The tip of the foot must still be visible in front of the knees. Tilt the pelvis forward. Back very straight, chin down, cervical spine straight. This is the basic state!
Hold your palms diagonally outwards at the level of the navel. Point your palm down to absorb earth energy.

Explanation of the exercise: This exercise regulates the energy flow of the whole body. You absorb the yin energy of the earth, raise your energy potential, bring your own energy to free circulation and regulate the respiratory tract, heart and circulation, digestive tract, inner glands and the nervous system. The exercise has a calming effect. Above all, the immune system is strengthened by increasing the energy potential.
Any slight spontaneous movements that may occur are normal; Muscle tremors can also occur all over the body. You start with 5 minutes a day. After 2 weeks you can increase by 5 minutes each. A calm, correspondingly long piece of music eliminates the need to look at the clock. Then walk around a bit.

4) Exercise for the Dai Mo (belt jar)

-With the palms down, towards the earth, describe circles next to the hip, breathe naturally

-Inhale while palms move to the navel and then to the hip

-Swipe your thumb back over the belt while bending your upper body back, stretch your buttocks forward

-Exhale as your palms move forward, while also bending your upper body.s.

Explanation of the exercise: In traditional Chinese medicine, the belt vessel is a meridian that flows through the pelvis like a belt and is used primarily for disorders such as pain during the day, irregular cycle, impotence, etc. The belt vessel wraps itself like a circle around the energy channels that flow up from the legs. If a blockage in the belt vessel is regulated, the energy also flows more freely in the other energy channels (e.g. cold feet should become warm).

1 Dai-Mo-Übung 2

3 4

5 6

7 8

5)Regulation of the triple heater meridian

The triple heater meridian coordinates the function of the various organs; it is superior in its function.

- Sedate (calm down); Take the basic position, one hand at the neck, the other hand at the abdomen at a distance of 5 cm from the body. Now the upper hand

- Palms facing the body - goes down on the body (without touching it), while the lower hand goes up on the outside. Then the upper hand goes down in the same way and the lower hand goes up, etc.

- Tonize (stimulate); Take the basic position, position of the hands as above, only now the lower hand, palm of the hand facing the body, at a distance of 5 cm from the body, slowly from bottom to top and the upper hand at the same time outside from top to bottom (vice versa as with sedation) .

- Explanation of the exercise: Sedate for all diseases in which an abundance is to be reduced, e.g. acute pain, severe flatulence, acute diarrhea, heartburn, bad breath, stomach pain. Toning for all diseases in which one wants to strengthen or stimulate, e.g. chronic complaints such as bloated belly, chronic Diarrhea, feeling cold.
Concentrate on the palms of your hands, check carefully what you feel in the abdominal area.

 - 14 times -

1 Dreierwärmer-Übung   2

3   4

6)Follow the flow of energy with a calming effect

- Relax, concentrate on the palms, breathe naturally

- Slowly raise both arms sideways, the palms facing down, absorb yin energy

- Turn your palms up at shoulder level, the palms absorb yang energy,

- Bend your arms in your elbows, hold your palms in front of your forehead for a moment without touching them, thereby giving your head clear energy

- Breathe in deeply, turn your palms horizontally to the ground as you exhale and slowly push them down along your body.a   .

Explanation of the exercise: Pathogenic energy or an abundance should be derived from the head downwards (as with the lightning rod). You should get a "cool head" again.
Effective for heart diseases, high blood pressure, nervousness, stress.
Not suitable for low blood pressure, anemia, low white blood cell count.

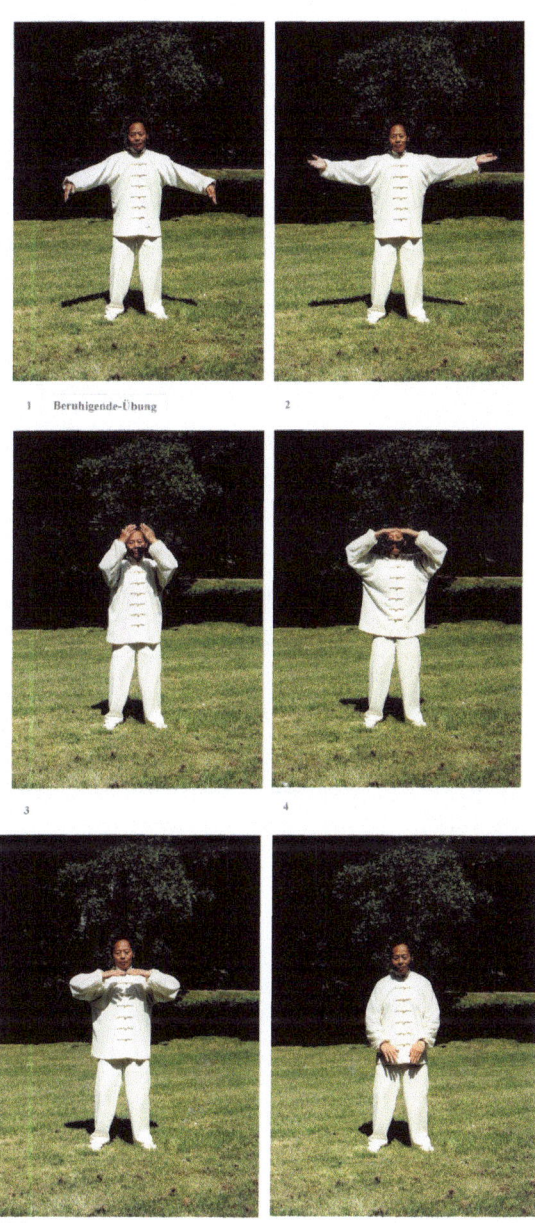

1   Beruhigende-Übung   2

3   4

5   6

7)Follow the energy flow with a stimulating effect

- Hold both palms up in front of your lower abdomen, fingertips do not touch.

- When inhaling, raise both palms up to the sternum, thinking that blood and energy flow up

- Slowly turn your palms towards your body, let your palms slide 5 cm away from your body (palm of your hand pointing towards your body) while exhaling, thinking that pathogenic energy is flowing downwards.

- Explanation of the exercise; Even if the palms of the hands only go to the breastbone, the energy flows to the head.
Exercise for low blood pressure, morning tiredness, anemia (anemia), low white blood cell count.
With high blood pressure no more than 7 times.
2 times a day 49 times with complaints.

1　Anregende-Übung　　　　　　　　2

3　　　　　　　　　　　　　　　4

8) Bring energy into free flow - release blockages

2 phases: a) lifting - lowering
              b) open - close

a) - When lifting the hands, think that earth energy is inhaled into the body through the palms of the hands and soles of the feet, up to a sick area - when exhaling, slowly lower your hands, thinking that pathogenic energy is drained through the point Ni 1, in a pit below the base of the toes under the sole of the foot, into the soil.
- Inhale when lifting - Exhale when walking down;

b) - When opening the hands, think that energy from outside flows into the skin pores of the body when inhaled and opened.

- As you exhale, approach your palms (do not touch them), thinking that all pathogenic energy is being pushed out of your body.
- Inhale when opening -Exhale when closing;
at least 7 times

Explanation of the exercise: This exercise releases energy blockages, it is therefore suitable for many chronic diseases. Above all, it is practiced in China at hospitals and at the Shanghai Research Institute in cancer and tumor follow-up groups; also effective for diabetes.

1   Energiefluß-Übung

2

3

4

5

6

9)Exercise to strengthen the spine

Basic position, but pushing through the knees, concentrating on the palms of the hands, swinging the arms naturally back and forth without force;
 - While the arms swing forward, bend your upper body slightly, stretch your buttocks backwards, inhale as you do so
- While the arms swing backwards, thrust out your stomach and buttocks and exhale.
Start slowly with spinal complaints, pay attention to the body. Slowly increase the speed.

Explanation of the exercise; The spine moves like a snake in this exercise. It strengthens the spine and is good for back pain. Yen Mo and Tou Mo, the two meridians that go through the middle of the body at the front and back, are flooded with energy.
-at least 14 times -

1   Wirbelsäulen-Übung

2

3

4

33

10) Exercise to strengthen the body's Yang energy

- Basic position, relax, breathe naturally

- Slowly raise both arms up to the shoulders, holding them out straight forward, hand hanging loosely in the wrist, bent downwards; inhale while doing so

- Suddenly jerkily stretch your hands and fingers upwards and pull them towards your head, holding out your arms and holding your breath

- Slowly lower both arms back to the starting position, exhaling as you do so

- Suddenly bend your arms, at the same time jerkily clench your hands into a fist and place them on your pelvic bones, inhaling quickly and vigorously, then hold your breath

- Exhale again and let your arms hang loosely

- Slowly raise your arms sideways to shoulder height; breathe in

- All of a sudden, jerkily stretch your hands upwards, continue to inhale quickly and vigorously, then hold your breath;

- Exhale, slowly lower your arms to the basic position

- Suddenly bend your arms, at the same time jerkily clench your hands into a fist and place them on your pelvic bones, inhaling quickly and vigorously, then hold your breath

- Exhale again and let your arms hang loosely

- Slowly raise your arms sideways to shoulder height; breathe in

-All of a sudden, jerkily stretch your hands upwards, continue to inhale quickly and vigorously, then hold your breath

-Exhale, slowly lower your arms to the basic position

- Suddenly bend your arms, at the same time jerkily clench your hands into a fist and place them on your pelvic bones, inhaling quickly and vigorously, then hold your breath

- Slowly lower both arms back to the starting position, exhaling as you do so.
This is a cycle - repeat.

--7 times-

Explanation of the exercise:

This exercise strongly stimulates blood circulation, releases blockages by making energy flow and flowing through all meridians and their branches. Effective especially when feeling cold, chronic rheumatism, fatigue and weakness.

1 Yang-Übung 2

3 4

5

6

7

8

11) Exercise to strengthen lung function

- Take basic position, hold both palms in front of the navel, concentrate on palms

- Slowly move both arms up and down in the opposite direction, breathing in

- Then suddenly a palm jerked up to the sky, fingers to the middle; the other palm down to the ground

-    ingers forward, stretching out forcefully, breathing in and holding more air. Inhale as you stretch to absorb yin and yang energy from the cosmos into the lung meridian

- Slowly move your arms back to the basic position, exhale for a long time, then change the right and left arm in the position and continue as above.

- at least 7 times-

Explanation of the exercise; This exercise strengthens the function of the lungs, the lungs are stretched and compressed like a bellows. Yin and Yang energy runs through the palms and arms in the lung meridian to the lungs. In patients with high blood pressure and heart disease a maximum of 7 times.

1 & 3 Lungen-Übung 2

4 5

12) "Arrow exercise"

- Place your left hand on the thigh of the angled left leg, right leg straight back. Right foot is at right angles to left foot. Right hand naturally hangs down

- Look at the inner surface of the right hand, slowly rotate your hand clockwise, breathe in from the front upwards, exhale backwards and downwards, while doing so it is very important in this exercise - looking at the inner surface of the circular hand judges.
Breathe in when lifting the arm, exhale when lowering
Make 7 circles with your right hand, then change your foot position and 7 circles with your left hand.
7 times the right hand, 7 times the left hand.

Explanation of the exercise: The energy circulation in the meridians of the hand is stimulated, the lungs are opened and pressed like a bellows.
Good for shoulder pain, cervical syndrome, lung complaints .

If you have a tendency to severe dizziness or a herniated disc of the cervical spine, you only look forward while the arm circles.

1   Pfeil-Übung

2

3

4

13) Exercise for the kidney meridian and cervical spine

- Basic position, relax, put both hands on the kidney region

- When inhaling, pull your chin towards your neck, at the same time bend your shoulders slightly forward

- Exhale, take your shoulders back, keep your head relaxed again, stretch your chin slightly forward.
2 times a day 49 times

Explanation of the exercise: The cervical spine is stretched during this exercise. Since according to traditional Chinese medicine the energy of the kidney meridian supplies the bones and especially the spine, energy is pumped up by the kidneys along the tou meridian to the head and spine.
Strengthens kidney function, good for cervical spine syndrome.

1 HWS-Übung

2

3

14) Exercise to stimulate the large meridian cycle

- Bend your knees and run your hands down along the outside of your legs, then up again on the inside of your legs, keeping your upper body straight, straightening up

- On the front of the body continue up to the neck, run your hands around your neck and place your hands on the cervical spine

- Now put your hands up at the back of your head, bring them down over your face to the middle of your breastbone, from there on over your lower rib cage to your kidneys, stay there for a moment, continue to your hips, then return to the basic position .

- Both hands touch the body directly from the beginning to the end of the exercise.
- 7 times -

Explanation of the exercise.This exercise stimulates energy circulation throughout the body and can release energy blocks.
It is effective for almost all chronic diseases and for feeling cold.
Not suitable for high blood pressure and severe organic heart problems (too strenuous).

1 Meridian-Massage-Übung   2

3   4

5   6

7   8

15)Exercise to strengthen metabolism and kidneys

Stand relaxed, feet together, palms together, lift up to head height, turn large circles, bend your knees and turn your hips in the opposite direction to your hands (e.g. hands are to the left, hips to the right). Keep torso straight; Exhale downward movement, inhale upward movement.
- Do the exercise slowly, turn at least 7 times to the right and 7 times to the left, but always the same number of times in each direction if it is carried out several times.
7 times on the right and 7 times on the left

Explanation of the exercise: Exercise to strengthen the kidneys and vital energy, stimulates the metabolism, good for losing weight - especially on the stomach and hips. Patients with high blood pressure and heart disease should not do this exercise too often.

1   Stoffwechsel-Übung   2

3   4

16) Exercise "Cloud Pushing"

- Stand relaxed, see picture 1, the weight is on the right foot with the right leg bent, left hand at shoulder height, right hand at navel height, palms facing away from the body.

- Then move to the left, with weight change to the left leg, then change hands, right hand is now up, left hand down, palms now face in the opposite direction, i.e. to the right; Weight shifts to the right leg, which is now angled. Slowly move the body while the hands go to the other side in front of the body (pushing a cloud in the imagination).

- In this way, move back and forth harmoniously and slowly from left to right and vice versa. Change hands and back. Both palms always point in the same direction of movement. The upper hand shows the direction of the movement. E.g. the right hand is at shoulder level: move to the right. Concentrate on the palms.
14 times, at least 7 times in each direction

Explanation of the exercise: Strengthens the circulation in all meridians, particularly effective for strengthening the lungs, legs and back.

1   Wolkenschieben

2

3

4

17) Exercise to strengthen the metabolism

- Sitting position, leaning your back against the wall so that 3 right angles are closed. 90 ° arise

- Hold your palms about 10 cm in front of your upper abdomen.
2 minutes, at least until the legs start to shake.

Explanation of the exercise; Gastric, liver and Pancreatic meridians flow from the toes to the corresponding metabolic organs. Pressure on the toes and muscle tension in the thighs stimulate circulation and energy flow, particularly in these meridians.

The exercise is effective and regulates stomach and gastrointestinal complaints, obesity on the abdomen and thighs and serves to strengthen health in general. (According to a study of 3,000 students in Shanghai, weight loss was recorded in 87.6% of cases after 2 months with once-daily exercise and normal eating habits.)
Not suitable for patients with high blood pressure and serious heart diseases.

1   Magen-Abnehm-Übung   2

3

18)Circling the hip

-Basic status, relax, focus on navel.
Let the region circle between the hip and navel
(as with belly dancing), keeping your upper
body and legs straight.
49 times - alternating to the right and to the left.

Explanation of the exercise; According to the
Qigong teaching, an energy reserve is stored in
the solar network. This exercise mobilizes this
reserve of energy.
Effective for back pain, stiffness in the back
area. Also recommended for strengthening the
abdominal organs.

1 Hüftkreisen

2

3

Energy intake in the 3 dantiane

- Basic position at the window or facing the trees, relax,
Slowly raise arms sideways (1)

- Delivering energy from the environment to the lower Dantian point (2 cm below the navel) with a sweeping, embracing movement, inhaling. Linger for a moment with your palms towards your body (without touching it) and concentrate on the triangle palms-Dantian (2)

- Bring your hands down parallel to your body, exhale

- Return to the basic position, after a long embracing movement (as above), stay with the middle Dantian (middle sternum) (3)

- Bring your hands down parallel to your body and exhale

- Return to the basic position, exercise as above, then stay in front of the upper Dantian (middle of the forehead, between the eyebrows) (4)

- Bring your hands down parallel to your body and exhale

During the exercises, the body should resonate with the hand movements.

Explanation of the exercise: Energy from the cosmos is absorbed in 3 energy centers.
7 times -

1   Dreifache Energieaufnahme   2

3   4

20) Cleaning exercise

In some places you don't feel well, some people exhaust you or you have a bad feeling in your body. When you leave you feel better. Why? Wasted or bad energy. There are 2 types, on the one hand the bad energy in a sick body, on the other hand the pathogenic energy in the air, e.g. through pollution. This bad energy can be removed by the following exercise. It is called "washing bone marrow" and is carried out as follows:

-Feet shoulder width, parallel, arms stretched out, palms down (absorb earth energy), at shoulder level: turn hand (absorb sky energy) and inhale with all movement.

-Guide palms to the head and exhale. One should imagine that the collected energy flows into the back of the head and then into the cervical spine.

-Then you raise your hands a little, inhale, lower your hands towards your head, exhale and imagine sending the energy from the thoracic spine to the lumbar spine.

-You raise your hands again a little, inhale and then lower your hands in front of and to the side of your body to the floor and crouch, accompanied by the idea that the good energy presses the used and bad energy from the lumbar spine to the legs into the ground.

-From the crouching position on the ground, jump up, raise your arms and hit them standing, landing against the ground, shouting "Tschö" and giving up used and bad energy.
3 times

1 Reinigungsübung

2

3

4

5

6

7

8

21) General final exercise

After the Qigong exercises, a strong energy field
was built up in and around the hands. Therefore,
as a conclusion of the exercises: first hold one
minute around the navel, then close your hand to a
fist, rub your hands against each other and pass on
the remaining energy, e.g. on the face (reduces
wrinkling) or on the hands or over a sick organ or
a sick part of the body.

Also from the same author:

Qi Gong sitting ISBN 9783750431409

This book describes 34 Qi Gong exercises performed while sitting. From simple movement exercises to Tuina massage exercises, breathing exercises and concentration exercises. These exercises improve the energy intake, strengthen the self-healing powers and balance the autonomic nervous system. They promote the ability to concentrate and inner peace. They have a positive effect on the digestive system, the muscles, the tendons, joints and the spine. The increased oxygen intake strengthens the heart and lungs.

It is very well suited as a exercise book for occupational medicine, for old people's home, as a completion for any Qi Gong course or just for in between for all office or computer workers. The many photos and the clear description make it easy to understand the exercises.

Taiji Qi Gong in 22 Steps ISBN:9783752820072

In this book there are 22 Taiji Qi Gong exercises described. These exercises improve energy intake, strengthen the self-healing powers and bring about a balance of the vegetative nervous system. They promote concentration and inner peace. They have a positive effect on the digestive organs, the muscles, the tendons, joints and the spine. The increased oxygen intake strengthens the heart and lungs.

Available soon:

Qi Gong standing exercises

This book describes 23 Qi Gong standing exercises. These exercises improve energy intake, strengthen the self-healing powers and balance the vegetative nervous system. You promote the ability to concentrate and inner peace. They strengthen the muscles and tendons. The standing positions of the 5 animals (monkey, deer, bear, tiger, crane) are also suitable for children.